the
freedom
of
forward

For Sarah

Table of Contents

Preface

Those on their journey of healing and growth often seek and appreciate words of wisdom yet seldom understand the depth of the wounds that had to exist for that wisdom to mature or the scars and thorns that still remain to inspire today's testimonies.

The same strongholds that crippled and condemned me also inspired and ignited my creativity.

And although poetry, prose, and a unique perspective grew from the fruits of my frustrations, life experiences, inner work, and faith…my failure to uproot seeds of suffering, strife, self-criticism, and sadness only left room for negative self-talk, irrational fear, doubt, and pain to blossom.

This led to me becoming my own roadblock on my journey.

I found myself walking in what I had prayed and prepared for, grateful for every ordered step and stop that directed me thus far yet unsettled. Knowing in my heart that something was missing; better yet, I was harboring something that didn't belong.

I was making external strides, glowing, growing, and thriving but internally the impact was stunted because my mind was not completely free of the shackles I allowed to be placed upon it.

Fixating on, fearful of, and flustered by what I couldn't control, acknowledge, release, or forget. Tired of holding on to what was never meant for me to carry, yet too accustomed to its presence to easily release.

Acknowledging our need to let go, stand in our truth, move forward, and pivot is only one component of the healing process. Giving ourselves the permission, grace, time, and space to do so is another.

It's a process that requires us to be self-aware and willing to identify and address what is holding us back and make peace with what once left us in pieces as we discover gratitude in the broad view. A view that reveals the most authentic, empathetic, wise, and impactful versions of ourselves.

The format and tone of this book will allow readers to dive into the internal conflict and monologue one experiences as they fully surrender and seek total healing. Combatting pride, people-pleasing, trauma, condemnation, resentment, and offense, this read will uncover the contrast of flesh-led and spiritually-led thoughts that one experiences when shifting their mindset and highlight its impact on our identity, spiritual health, mental wellness, and overall well-being.

Intertwining words of wisdom, raw revelations, honest reflections, spiritual truths, and writings of hope and encouragement, the following pages penned are the sounds of my soul, the fruit of my faith, records of my renewed mindset and purpose executed in paragraph form.

May you not only accept that every experience and emotion endured in your life is valid and your truth is unshakable, but also identify the impact and importance of embracing your truth, finding freedom in forgiveness, standing firm in self-love, fostering your focus and faith in God, and releasing what no longer serves you.

5

Introduction

*Even if your tears teach you and the strengths revealed work
together and stay, if you don't release the burdens and bruising
that your mind, body, and spirit encountered on your journey –
you will not feel free.*

Life is filled with profound lessons if we make the choice to
humble ourselves and learn from every path we've taken,
pressure that propelled us, and darkness that shined on our true
essence.

Through reflection and reframing, we are able to identity not
only what truly matters but also what stands in the way of us
being our most authentic, healed, and whole self. There is a
heaviness that persists when we can't release people-pleasing,
offense, unforgiveness, condemnation, and resentment. Silent
roots that only cultivate suffocating fruits of fear, anxiety, regret,
and anger.

Before we can *joyfully* mentally, spiritually, and emotionally
move **forward** with confidence, inner peace, and a greater
appreciation of who we are and the testimony we've earned,
we must *genuinely* acknowledge the **feelings** and footholds that
impact our mindset, heart, faith, and perspective.

By addressing the internal obstacles that make forgiving
ourselves, others, and the past seem unattainable, we can reframe
and release what is hindering us from healing our deepest hurts,
as we progress in our purpose and indulge in the **freedom** of
letting go of what's behind and embracing what is and what is to
come.

Healing requires you to show the lowest version of yourself the highest amount of accountability, understanding, compassion, and love.

Suppressed emotions, unexpressed offenses, and unmet expectations led to some of the heaviest and most needless weights I've ever carried in life.

Frozen, yet enlightened through the emotions, exposure and lessons I once experienced concurrently...I acquired beautiful insights all while blindly accumulating issues with them. Issues that didn't internally present themselves until the struggles passed but the suffering didn't.

Though *still* in obedience, in my silence I gained priceless revelation and wisdom, but it also cost me the comfort and confidence in using my voice.

I allowed the opinions and optics of others to overshadow the truth of my reality as my desire to just let the storms pass led me to drowning in the depression of each raindrop and teardrop that I felt. I allowed my own insecurities and internal conflicts to shift my view of life and myself which led me to see through the lens of only seeking protection and peace – overanalyzing everything and everyone along the way.

By knowingly and unknowingly putting my pain, pressures, and problems on a pedestal, I consequently dragged my heart, hope, and happiness on the floor.

Although I know I am free, it is time to fully embody my freedom. Moving every mountain that has long resided in my mind, I am consciously and graciously making room for every blessing, aspect of growth, and inner healing that I was born to receive. I am embracing the freedom of moving forward.

the freedom of forward

PART I:
FEELING

The deepest thorns in your side stem
from the expectations of others and yourself
that were never met,
the words that you left unspoken,
and the battles you silently fought.

I can't move forward until I acknowledge
that pain not only existed but also impacted me
in ways far beyond eyes could ever see
or my lips would ever allow me to admit.

Sometimes, the obstacle standing in your way is you.

It is the avoidance, anger, and apprehension to put all that hurt you behind you that is restricting you from moving forward.

It is your inability to let go of the past and your routine to relive it every day in the present that is draining you.

It is your inner child or former self that is fearful of speaking up – because you know it can reopen a wound you don't want to deal with – that leads your suffering to scream within the confines of your mind.

It is your fear of being hurt, mishandled, or betrayed again that leads you to limit the amount of love both sent and received.

You are not unworthy of inner freedom.
The issue is that it feels unnatural
for you to receive it.

A weight comes when you hold on to anything that isn't naturally connected to you mentally, spiritually, emotionally, or physically.

A weight that seemingly takes your breath away with each step forward and makes your journey tiring and tormenting as you come to accept that depletion stems from being unwilling to release an attachment that was never yours to pick up.

That is what shame, condemnation, unforgiveness, and bitterness will do.

The longer you hold it, the heavier it gets.

You must do this for yourself.

Place one foot in front of the other as you make the conscious decision to release the grip that anger has on you, replacing it with a level of grace you would desire God to grant.

Forgive yourself and others in hopes of achieving a freedom yet to be experienced and a peace that surpasses all understanding.

Moving forward does not mean you are denying the past, its pains, and pressures ever existed. It simply means you are choosing to focus on and carry forward the insights, experiences, and awareness they have provided.

It was real.

Everything you experienced and
every emotion you endured was real.

Even if no one asked.
Even if no one believed.
Even if no one protected you.
Even if you kept a brave face,
and no one realized you were crumbling.

It was real.
All of it.

And because it was real,
because it altered your view of yourself,
the world and the people around you,
because it altered the way you think, live, and communicate,
because it made you question your sanity, safety, and strength...
you must give yourself permission to truly acknowledge, release,
and heal from it.

I did more than allow hard times,
sharp words, outside opinions,
and unmet expectations to impact me.

I allowed them to overpower my inner voice,
become a breeding ground for my insecurities,
and impact my identity.

One of the greatest torments I've ever inflicted on myself was mentally replaying and constantly remembering the details, emotions, and words associated with the times that shook, offended, and hurt me most.

I thought it was protecting me;
but, all it did was punish me further.

You can downplay your pain
to everyone who crosses your path
and convince them that something
is not bothering you.

But, you can never truly fool yourself,
your spirit, or your nervous system.

I was so concerned with
who you thought I was,
that I lost sight of
who I truly am.

A broken record skipping and scoring
with every trigger that presented itself.

Frozen, flustered, and frustrated:
silent in my suffering and strife.
Meditating on and being tormented by
all that brought me pain, yet too accustomed
to its impact to remember that I have
and could live without it.

I felt I had lost a piece of myself.
The part of my personality and outlook that had so much
wonder, optimism, and hope. The part of me that believed
everything and everyone was inherently good.

The part of my heart that trusted and extended without fear and
truly, yet foolishly believed all I was exposed to was all there
was.

Those rose-colored glasses kept me naive, but ignorance kept me
in bliss.

And ever since I've taken them off, seeing all components of my
life and myself as is and became aware of the darkness in the
world – I find myself hiding from it.

Depressed, apprehensive, and holding tightly to what light and
security I have left.

I pray you heal from the hurts deeply rooted within your mind, yet have never been spoken from your mouth.

I pray the scales are removed from your eyes so conviction can one day take up the space that chaos now has in your life.

I pray you allow yourself to tap into the goodness within your heart and begin to intentionally appreciate the good people in your life.

May every broken piece within you be used to create the most beautiful masterpiece of redemption, resilience, and righteousness you have ever seen and align with an amount of peace you have yet to experience.

It's heavy,
it's hurting,
and it's time
to put it down.

You've carried it,
overcompensated because of it
and allowed it to rob you of your peace
long enough.

The past was never meant
to occupy this space in the present
or rend you fearful of the future.

Heal the hurt you've put effort into hiding
and address the core of what is truly affecting you.

You don't need to know how God will do it.
Merely have faith and trust that He will.

Your anxiety will not expedite a single ordered step,
but your obedience will keep you covered.

It is easy to tell someone
to let go of something
because it's been so long
when you don't understand
the amount of time it took
that person to heal from it
or how much that pain still
affects them today.

I experienced every reaction
when it came to pain in my life.
I ran from it. I fought it.
I froze when triggered by it.

But as time, acceptance, and understanding ensued,
I realized I'd never truly heal and move on from the pain
until I acknowledged its presence and later gave it
permission to leave.

There is wisdom
in those wounds
and a story behind
your silence.

It hurt and traumatized me more
than I expressed to anyone else.
More than I was willing to accept
within myself.

It shook, changed, and impacted
my mind, life, and hope in ways
I didn't feel I ever truly put back together.

And maybe that was the point of it all.

More than anyone else's
love, support, and trust,
I needed my own.

I needed to know who I was
even if no one else did.

I needed to see the beauty
in all that I was
and all that I wasn't,
especially in times when the world
seemed ugly and I felt hidden
or misunderstood by everyone in it.

I wouldn't have ever truly identified
and embraced the woman in the mirror
if I didn't experience the darkness with her.

The peak would be meaningless without memories in the pit.

I wouldn't appreciate my joy, laughter, and life to the extent I
now do had I not wiped my own tears, picked myself off the
ground, and worked on myself from the inside out.

Had I not delved deeper into my problems, pressure, and
passions, I would have never been propelled and uniquely
positioned into my purpose.

In life we will all struggle, overcome obstacles, and live to experience times that leave us to question everything about ourselves, our lives, and the people we allowed in it.

But how we react and what we make of our hills and valleys will have the influence to lead us in two vastly different directions: pain-stricken or purpose-driven.

What we allow to prune and preserve us is what will reflect the most about our heart posture and character.

My depression increased when I began
to see and accept life as it was
versus as I expected or imagined.

When I began to understand that I'm not perfect
and there were areas I needed to grow and outgrow.

When I learned the hard way that I could be friends
with people who are not friends to me.

High functioning does not mean *not struggling*.
Keeping a brave face does not conquer
the chaos within you or calm the storms around you.

Yet somehow, we've convinced ourselves suffering
in silence is an attribute of those who are strong.
Falling apart from the inside out is fine
as long as you are well put together externally.

Even worse is that because we believe silencing our struggles is
strength, we fool ourselves into believing that
asking for help, acknowledging our own toxicity, and holding
people accountable is weakness.

For years, I lived in a constant state of anxiety.
Crippled with fear, meditating on the words of others,
and replaying the pains of my life.

Wrapped with a smile, gentle embrace, and achievements,
I was healed and hurting. I was free but fighting my own
thoughts.

the freedom of forward

It's painful yet profound what hurt can do to a person.
How going through the most tumultuous times of your life
will not only leave you with life lessons but also great losses.

Losses that are not apparent until
you reach for trust, security, and optimism
and they are no longer there.

You took your persona off the pedestal
and put your pain on it.

Leading you to meditate on
the peace and people you lost
instead of appreciating the maturity
and mindset you gained.

I want to fully forgive and forget.

But no matter how much time passes,
divine confirmation comes,
or how many prayers are prayed,
I still find myself hurting.

Offended, condemned, and dumbfounded –
wishing it could have gone differently
and wanting to let the shackles
that suffering left me with – go.

God, I wish I could see what you see:
the heart of man, the purpose behind every pressure,
and the magnitude that discovering
our identities in you possesses.

I try with everything in me to drown out the sound
of any doubts that linger
and embrace the fact that you hold
the ability to know far beyond
what I can even imagine.

But I struggle.

Even on days that I operate as a vessel,
I can find myself thirsting to fully receive it.

Not because I don't believe you,
but because there are times
I struggle to fully believe in myself.

There is no person on this planet who has been more condescending, crueler, and callous toward me than myself.

No person who made me question my identity and insult me more than the person who stares back at me in the mirror.

I thought it was conviction and accountability trying to make me grow up until I realized the extent of mental torment I was consistently serving myself, in addition to self-loathing and condemnation, was only keeping me down.

I cared so much about people's opinions
and carried the shame of what they boldly
yet blindly believed to the point I created
walls that not only kept them out
but also kept me isolated.

I used to pray memories would just fade,
the anger would wash away,
and I could go back to being the less aware
yet optimistic person I was before.

No, I didn't have as much wisdom,
but I believe I had more comfort.

The person who saw the good in people, entrusted everyone on
face value until I learned I shouldn't. The one with the old soul
yet childlike zest and love for life.

I wish I could reset the part of me that is now so selective
I'd rather be alone.

I condemned you mercilessly.
Blaming you for every problem
and highlighted your lack to the point
that you lost sight of your light.

You lost the volume in your voice.
You lost the ability to identify
and embrace who you truly are.

I punished you by putting you down and convinced you to reject
any compliments, love, or encouragement you received as I used
crushing yet cunning arguments to do so.

Whispering imaginations into your ears saying, "Yes, those
people know and love you, but they don't really know you. They
don't see how flawed you are or how insecure you can be. They
don't hear how you speak to yourself in the pits of your pain.
They see the smile on your face, not the tongue you're biting
behind it."

I reminded you of every "should have" and "could have" of your
life. I led you to view every new experience through the lens of
"what if", "but last time", "I'm not good enough", or "I'm not
safe".

And even when God confirmed, then reminded you, He saw it
all, He knows, and that you are forgiven, I made a point that you
wouldn't forget so you could never fully move on without the
weight, worry, and wounds.

Fear has had an unnecessary yet immeasurable impact on my life and has manifested in a multitude of forms.

Whether it was paranoia, anxiety, self-sabotage, or self-loathing, I allowed my feelings, fears, and frustrations to create a barrier that only myself and God could break.

Shame, irrational fear, and condemnation
will create "what if" scenarios that make no sense,
yet seamlessly validate the argument
insecurity presents within your mind.

It is a constrictor, squeezing the life out of you
with every breath you take.

The pain controlled my mind
to the point my thoughts
wouldn't stop racing
and controlled my tongue
to the point I said nothing.

It's safe to say that much of my people-pleasing stemmed from my inability to understand and stand on the truth of who I actually was.

I didn't recognize my power, so I gave it away in the form of overreacting, over-analyzing, and overcompensating.

The world will clip your wings,
then question why you no longer
have the desire or ability to fly.

I lacked self-confidence and carried inner shame
to the extent that the sound of other people's words
and feelings towards me echoed louder in my mind
than the facts of my experiences and the truth
of who I truly was.

How can no one see?
How is no one catching on?

How do people sit back, open their mouths,
and firmly believe they know more about
your suffering, success, experiences, or emotions
than you do?

Even without asking
or trying to hear you...
how does that happen?

How is it more common than it is corrected?

It's over.

So, why am I still replaying
my suffering like a rerun?

Holding on to every detail
as clear as if it were yesterday?

You'd think it would be easier
to just put it all behind me,
but its impact is complex.

It's changed how I viewed everything:
the world, people, and the idea of who I am.

The person I am most apprehensive of
is not merely the one who has made poor choices
or has hurt others.

We have all done that and are capable of doing so.

It's the person who habitually inflicts pain and disorder who
has the ability to identify the negative impact their words
and actions have on others; yet, lacks the remorse, conviction,
and willingness to change.

You enjoyed that, didn't you?
Spewing sharp words in hopes
of a reaction from me.
Finding delight in my depression,
opportunity in those who envy,
and conversation of my crumbling.

How exhilarating, yet exhausting it must be
to sow webs with such deception...
stabbing people in the back
while seemingly harmless
in front of everyone's face.

The energy it takes to be the victim,
the hero, the aggressor, and the desired
takes effort I'd imagine.
But, that's your gift isn't it?

After all, you seem to exert it so well.

Masking and making it your mission
to convince people you're real and confident,
all while doing the fakest and weakest things.

Hurting people you know would never
go out of their way to hurt you back,
all while cunningly convincing others
that who you hurt deserved it.

I've learned not to judge books by their covers
when the moral of the stories they left me with
taught me the importance of discernment.

Some of the most evil people I've ever encountered
have many friends and notable influence,
while some of the most genuine people I've ever met
have been outcasted and misunderstood.

And isn't that the irony of it all?

That people are not always who they post
or position themselves to be.

It's who they are underneath it all.

Who they are when no one is watching.
Who they are at heart.

I had so many unexpressed offenses and pent-up anger,
I told myself it was best to leave everything
and everyone alone.

Let them be wrong, get myself right,
and never look back.

No explanation, no clarification,
no conversation – just distance, development, and done.

When a person is committed
to misunderstanding you and determined
to confirm whatever bias they have towards you,
oftentimes engaging with them comes to reveal
the trap for yourself.

MORGAN RICHARD OLIVIER

If you want vindication,
stand up and speak.
If you want information,
sit back and listen.

It's amazing the opinions and narratives
you can create from optics
and the community you can cultivate
from your bruised ego and bias.

Because that is the peak of your power, isn't it?

Draining the life, direction, and sanity out of people
you so badly wish you could further mishandle,
manipulate, or mold.

The people who know better.
The people who told you no.

The people who see you for what
and who you truly are.

MORGAN RICHARD OLIVIER

I was disgusted by you.

I hated the fact that your malice
made me want to cut the kindness
I had for myself and the love
I so genuinely shared with others
because no one and nothing
seemed safe anymore.

I couldn't believe in anyone –
including myself.

Patience, long-suffering, restraint, and the calm acceptance of revelation always seems to be perceived as weakness to people who do not possess those strengths.

It comes off as not being able to stand up for yourself, proof of guilt in some cases, or the lack of personal power. When it is the exact opposite.

Wisdom reminds us that if we can't control our minds, mouth, and movements, then we will struggle to manage our lives, the opportunities we are aligned for, and people we are meant to cross paths with.

Sometimes, the most difficult
yet intelligent choice to make
is to operate out of wisdom;
not out of what is perceived as right.

You may have all the receipts, honesty, and room
in the world to speak a truth that is on your heart.

But, if your intention is to avenge yourself and reveal
someone else while God has instructed you to be still,
then your motives are not pure and your efforts
will be out of order.

You'd be surprised by the amount
of pain and disappointment you're willing
to tolerate and not address when you are
exhausted, vulnerable, or seeking revelation.

It's the words I didn't speak
that taunted, haunted,
and tormented me most.

The points I didn't prove
in an effort to keep the peace
around me that led to
the longest most brutal wars
within me.

The anger I didn't act upon
that rattled me from within.

I buried my emotions, my truth, and my fight
and from there my bitterness, my fear,
and my distrust began to blossom.

You've never removed yourself from a table, friendship, or community out of the need for control or to teach anyone a lesson.

But you have quietly stopped all communication, removed yourself from environments, and completely cut ties with people when you felt unsafe, abused, or misled.

The problem with silence, absence, and avoidance is because there is no clarity or conversation, people who spectate will fill in the silence and space with whatever assumption, theory, or their own projections that can fit.

And as much as you feel your distance is a fortress, over time, if you don't heal and protect your mental health and inner voice, that fortress will slowly turn into a prison.

A safe cell that keeps you bound without chains being attached to you.

I learned to stop talking when I accepted
that I was not being listened to, asked,
believed, or genuinely considered.

When I realized giving my energy, access, and vulnerability to
anyone who was dead set on their view or assumptions was not
only foolish but also futile…I decided not to cast my pearls
before anyone who didn't deserve them and instead use the sting
of that hurt to aid in my healing.

Because a truth not accepted or asked for
does not minimize its validity, credibility, or soundness.

No matter how much time passes,
the truth **never** expires.

Shame and mental torment can lead you
to not standing up or defending yourself –
even when you hold the truth –
because although what the world is spreading
about you is not accurate, the hate and insults
they are spewing at you is what you feel
and speak within yourself.

I refuse to be present or vulnerable in spaces
where I'm not truly seen or safe.

That doesn't mean I'm causing division.
That doesn't mean I'm holding a grudge.
That doesn't mean I lack love for anyone.

That means I am respecting my discernment.

That simply means I'm protecting my peace,
upholding my boundaries and standing on
the wisdom I have acquired.

You don't hate them,
but you see them clearly.
You won't hurt them back,
but you will not allow them
to continue hurting you.

You get to a point that you protect yourself in the form of
removing access, energy, and attention. You lose the desire to
engage, converse, or reconnect which results in you eventually
removing yourself from the equation.

And as much as our generation prides itself on cutting people
off, many do not understand the pain that leads to that action and
the pain that follows – especially when you love people.

Self-isolating, detaching, and removing – although a form of
self-love and protection – is also your response to trauma and
stress. This response stems from not trusting people, not being
willing to let yourself be let down for the umpteenth time and
feeling it is safer and wiser to figure everyone out and fight on
your own because life has taught you that you are the only one
you can truly trust and depend on.

You would rather be alone, suffering in silence and build
yourself back up piece-by-piece than be around anyone you
believe would put you in that position, would add to it, or enjoy
seeing you in it.

People put titles over bullet holes
and expect the bleeding to stop.

Using a range of generic phrases such as:
...but they're family.
...but what will people think?
...be the bigger person.
...you've known each other for too long.
...it's going to bring division to the group.

These statements only add insult to injury.

It does not matter if a person is a relative by blood or by law.
It does not matter if you've known someone for much of your
life or have acquired memories over an extended period of time.

Your mental health, spiritual wellness, and overall well-being is
not about them. It is not about their optics, opinions, or what
excuse makes it easier for them to receive.

It's about protecting yourself, preserving your purpose, and
having peace within you.

You do not have to put yourself in a position to be consistently
hurt or abused to prove you are a good or loving person.

You can love those who hurt you and still have enough love for
yourself to release them, whether others agree with your stance
or not.

When you feel unseen, unheard, or misunderstood,
it seems like second nature to convince yourself
to struggle silently.

It seems wiser, safer, and easier to navigate alone.

When you feel that your words will be misinterpreted or
mishandled, of course you lose the desire to share them.

The saddest and most damaging decision most of us make is
discounting, diminishing, or diluting the truth of who we are or
the truth of our experiences because the lies around us led us to
believe the truth within us won't be believed or accepted.

It is at that point your silence is more than a muzzle that keeps
you miserable. Your silence is a mask that not only hides the
hurt but also hinders you from healing it.

The ones who I wanted
to support me most
taught me that I didn't need
any of their support to thrive.

You're going to be okay without them.

I know it seems wrong, uncomfortable, and even unfair at times that you must leave certain friendships, family members, and bonds behind because you've known and loved them for so long.

There is history there, memories that won't be forgotten and you've even made plans for them to be in your future.

At this present moment, in this season of your life, you must release the fact that you know them and carry yourself in a manner reflecting you now know better.

You know better than to be close to anyone who has repeatedly shown you they do not have your best interest or loyalty at heart.

You know better than to shrink yourself or question the validity of the evolution that took place within you because they refused to respect it or even acknowledge it.

Not everyone who starts the journey with you
is meant to make it to your destination.

Better yet, not everyone is sent, assigned, or aligned to you.

Some of the most misunderstood and mishandled people are those who detach instead of defending.

Those who seek isolation without offering the world an explanation. Those who keep their truth, pain, and business to themselves because they are exhausted and know the outcome would not be favorable by sharing it with someone who wouldn't understand or try to.

For a person to feel they aren't safe to seek the counsel or comfort from the people around them or are scared to let their guard down – cutting ties and access from those who are knowingly and unknowingly hurting them is painful, but feeling vulnerable, attacked, and discarded is excruciating.

People who love deeply
always end up suffering the longest
because they lead with the tenderness
of their heart and have a hard time
wrapping their minds around
the actions of anyone who doesn't.

the freedom of forward

My unconditional love for people
has hurt me more
than hatred ever could.

Being there for the sake of family
or staying there for the principle of friendship,
no matter the treatment or energy I received,
has undoubtedly developed my character;
yet, ultimately drained any ounce of desire
to be around them further.

Not because my love for them has waned
but because my level of tolerance
for needless pain has.

If you mean me no good,
please leave me alone.

I won't return or match your energy.
I won't talk about you…
especially if I'm not talking to you.

I say this not to reject you,
but to protect myself.

If you can't contribute to the peace
I have in my life,
by all means,
do not disturb it.

You can prove your loyalty to a person, support them through thick and thin, and love them with a fierceness that can't be ignored or disputed – and they will love you and all that you provide.

When the season shifts and you finally expect and need that energy, effort, and allegiance reciprocated to you in your time of suffering or success, do not be surprised if that person does not show it.

You calling to their memory all you genuinely did, all the love you consistently showed, and the hurt and confusion you feel because you aren't receiving it will cause them to look you in your face and boldly say, *"But I never asked you to."*

As much as your feelings are valid and you want to lash out, the only person you can be angry with is yourself.

Chances are, you expected something they not only never showed you they could provide or even desire to give but also something they never gave themselves.

You are crazy, guilty, not worthy of being considered,
or completely out of line – until they get a taste of what
they've been serving you.

Until it is their turn to feel alone or overwhelmed.
Until it is their turn to be lied to or lied about.
Until it is their turn to be mistreated or manipulated.
Until it is their turn to be some variation of you in the equation.

It isn't until then they even consider that perhaps you weren't the
sole source of the problem after all. Perhaps, what they said was
not what you lived or spoke. Perhaps, it all should have been
handled differently.

Maybe your perspective was worth seeking. Maybe you did have
something to say. Maybe the way you were treated wasn't
necessary. Maybe the disregard they had for you wasn't
deserved.

The sad part is, by the time that point comes, you likely won't
want to repair or regain anything that was lost. Not because you
don't want reconnection, vindication, unity, harmony, or any
other construct that you once desired, prayed for, or waited on.

But because you've seen and experienced too much to come
close to ever experiencing it again.

You've since put the pieces of your life back together. And
because you know just how much it took to learn, heal, and
move forward – you accept that you've come too far to return to
anyone or anything that broke you.

Your lack of energy and access to me
does not indicate I have a lack of love for you.

The separation and space between us
is for my safety and serenity; a reflection
of the lessons I've learned.

My intention is never to hurt anyone,
but I can no longer create opportunities
for hurt or hindrances to enter my life.

Extending forgiveness is one choice,
learning to not be a fool is another.

When you fully understand and accept
you are entitled to nothing in life,
it becomes easier to lose expectations
of others in many ways.

Not because you don't believe
in the goodness of people,
but because you understand the power
of your own choices and self.

I still love you.
I still want what's best for you,
and I still seek to see the best in you
like I always did.

But, I've come to accept
the fact that those feelings, motives,
and levels of love are not mutual.

I respect your choice,
even if you don't choose me.

I accept your opinions and feelings,
even if they do not align with who I am.

I've wasted enough time hoping you'd see me
or receive the words I've shared all this time.

I no longer concern myself
with who I can lose at this point.
I simply refuse to lose my focus, faith,
or myself ever again.

You've given enough energy and attention,
hoping they would see you.

Now, it's time to stop overlooking the importance
of protecting, loving, and embracing yourself.

For a long time, I cried and bargained with God
because I was so angry, isolated, and unsure of why He
separated me. Why I felt I was being rejected or misunderstood.

I later realized I was fighting Him to go back to a place, spaces,
and friendships where I never truly belonged.

I prayed He'd remove anything in me that was not right and were
a hinderance to His plan or His will. Yet, when He did, I got
depressed, insecure, and isolated myself.

I was a person who was having their prayers answered; yet,
consistently perceived them as another storm.

I thought if I prayed without ceasing, did everything I possibly could, and had my heart in the right place, it would change. Dysfunction would be fixed and all would be redirected to proper order. Wounds would be healed and wisdom would flourish. There would be harmony, a proven positive outcome to my unwavering hope, and the heaviness I felt would have no place in my life anymore.

That didn't happen.
Nothing around me changed,
but everything within me did.

There came a point where I had to accept that I simply couldn't do it anymore. I didn't want to feel anxious, alone, or alienated another day. I was tired of putting my efforts, energy, and attention into hurts and humans God told me to take my hands off long ago. I learned that ordered stops were just as important as ordered steps if I wanted to move forward in serenity and walk in my purpose.

So, I chose to release.
Not because I was giving up on anyone I love or myself.
But because I was fully giving it to God
and pressing on with peace.

With the hook of insults and insecurity,
offense baited me in, while pride kept me bound.

Sinking in burdens I was never meant to have and anchored to
anxiety that stemmed from ambiguity, I became angry, avoidant,
and alienated from the version of myself that was once free and
flowing through life with joy.

I was drowning in depression, torn to pieces because I could no
longer trust. I was sinking in suffering, not only did I fear
extending love but isolated myself fearing more fake love being
sent to me.

That is no way to live and only leads to the death of your joy,
mind, and heart posture. So, I cast it away.

Freeing my net of resentment, bitterness, and offense, choosing
to swim in the soothing rivers of wisdom, forgiveness, and
insight.

Those frustrations were allowed because they connected me to
gaining the spiritual fruits of self-control, patience, and
gentleness.

God is the source
not the people He created.

People don't have to like you, see you, or respect you.
People don't have to believe you, protect you, or support you.

You are not here to please man.
You are here to please and serve God.

I know you love people, and you want to be loved by them.
I know you've been hurt by people who you would have done
anything in your power to help, but the truth remains that you are
not on this planet to satisfy them or be seen by them.

You are here because you have a purpose.
You are here because you are meant to be here.
You belong here, so stand truly, genuinely,
and authentically here.

I remember times of my life that I prayed for vindication, reconnection, or the chance to converse with certain people. Yet, when the opportunity came to clear the air or clear my name, I listened more than I spoke.

When I had a window to speak my truth, I heard their thoughts and kept the details to my testimony.

My side was not asked for or considered. I learned and lived to understand that inner peace is more powerful and impactful than outside vindication and validation will ever be.

I don't need to keep or return anyone to my life who I don't trust and feel safe or seen by, and I won't ever knowingly fight for mess or stress to be around me.

I embraced the power of simply *letting them*.

I let them think, say, believe, and carry on as they want to and likely would have continued to, regardless. And proceeded to walk the other direction with my own self-control, truth, and authenticity intact. I can't control how another person perceives me; I can only control how I carry myself.

God allows you to go through
all things with the intent for you
to know better and know Him better.

Not everyone will talk to you before boldly and carelessly talking about you. Not everyone will hear the volume behind your silence or consider the true meaning behind your distance.

Not everyone will believe you, console you, stand up for you or even stand beside you. Please know they don't need to.

Revelation is less about your feelings and those people. It's more about seeing and accepting the facts of reality, addressing yourself, and knowing how to properly position people and yourself after all is revealed.

You don't have to acknowledge all that you're aware of, but you need to apply the lessons and move accordingly.

The stumbling block in your life,
the detour on your journey,
and the chapter that you only read
to an aligned or selective few
was never meant to destroy you.

It was meant to redirect you and refine you.

Praying and preparing is one thing.

Having the ability to not be provoked,
pressured, or knocked out of position
when you have it is another.

the freedom of forward

.

PART II: FREEING

When you understand your purpose,
power, and impact in this world
you will move, react, and think differently.

You will not put yourself in a position
for your morals, character, or respect
to be compromised.

You will align yourself with those who genuinely
love you and desire what's best for you
as you distance yourself from those who do not.

Best of all, you will realize the approval, validation, and love
you need most is your own.

Many of your pains from the past are based solely
on how you choose to perceive them.

Don't look back with resentment saying look what they did or
didn't do, or look back with condemnation saying look what I
did or should have done.

Look back with peace and joy in your heart as you think about
what God did, as you appreciate how His mercy and grace turned
some of your greatest sufferings into the empathy and exposure
you needed to align with your greatest success.

Forgiving, I am.
Forgetful, I am not.
And that is where I struggle.

Just when I think I released it,
the memories swim across my mind
with the flood of emotions to follow.
Drowning me in thoughts of what happened
and capsized by what should have been.

Serving as a not-so-sweet reminder
that although I moved on,
I took the bitterness
of that burden with me.

No one gets away with anything.

It doesn't matter if their lies are believed by the world.
It doesn't matter if they insulted you in front of your face
or stabbed you behind your back.
It doesn't matter if it seems that everyone has turned against you.

No matter how much time passes, how it looks, or if you feel
justice was not adequately served, trust and believe we all reap
what we sow.

Everyone has to pay for their motives and movements.

Oh, how your words taunted me and convinced me I wasn't worthy of compassion and care; yet, deserving of chaos and cruelty. You replayed every detail of my greatest struggles, failures, and mistakes as you shackled me to a level of shame that was never mine to carry. I held my tongue as I held on to every insult, offense, and lie – as if they were my truth or somehow earned.

Because you convinced me no one would hear me, choose me, or ever be concerned, I was damaged, dumb, and done for. Everything was my fault, my problem, and mine to suffer alone.

When conviction and repentance should have been enough, Condemnation, you told me regret and inner criticism would forever be my portion. And even when what the world, my negative self-talk, and my resentment said wasn't right, you reassured me I should accept it because if I connected the dots deep enough or long enough, I could clearly see I deserved it.

So, I shrunk myself to fit the boxes created by people who never saw me. I began to view myself through the lens of their projection and my deepest regrets, wrongs, and ridicule.

The *should haves* and *could haves* woke me up every morning and tucked me in at night, as you stood there proud of the paralyzed version of myself I was slowly and silently becoming. Now, those seasons are over. My voice is not only proven powerful but also courageous and clear. Gone are the days that I allow your words of fear, guilt, and mental torment to overpower my faith, growth, and development. I'm starving the temptation of depression, anger, and anxiety you cunningly serve.

You have always been called, chosen, and capable;
created to thrive and plant seeds of peace,
purpose, and positivity into those who cross your path.

Now that you've uprooted guilt
and every seed intended to get in your way,
you will not only overcome
but also stand on the faith
that carried you every step of the way.

Only confidence resides where
condemnation once occupied.

God, help me to release the pain, offense, resentment, trauma, and condemnation that came with my life lessons.

Help me to stop focusing on the hurts I can't forget. Teach me to reframe them in a way that I look back grateful for your grace and mercy, joyful to have the wisdom and understanding that stayed behind.

Give me a peace that surpasses all understanding and a level of empathy and honesty that allows me to share my testimonies with those who need it.

Anger, bitterness, and unforgiveness have no room or permission in my life.

Fill my mind with focus and my heart with love, as you set my eyes on what is ahead of me.

At this point, it is not the pain that a person inflicted upon you that is leading you to not forgive, keeping you flustered at the very thought of the offense, or leading you to do better or prove a point in spite of them.

It is your own pride.

It is your desire to be vindicated, valued, or viewed as a person worthy of an apology that is keeping you from gaining your own closure.

Your mental, spiritual, and emotional freedom is not found in their acknowledgement of a wrong. It is found in your ability to release it.

If you were to remove unforgiveness, offense, bitterness, and worry from your mind, body, and spirit, how large of a hole would it leave?

How much space would you have for more personal growth, alignment, and self-care? How would your faith, view of self, and boundaries be impacted if you chose to start removing your own immaturity, toxicity, and strongholds?

Be intentional about your inner healing, inner voice, and environment. Audit your circle and be honest about the impact your environment has on you mentally, spiritually, and emotionally.

Make room for the blessings, peace, and joy you are attracting into your life by earnestly and honestly assessing and addressing your life.

Be sure you make room for abundance, deliverance, and gratitude to bloom.

On the other side of letting go
is the beauty of embracing
all you've made room for.

Life is ironic, isn't it?

We don't appreciate joy until we truly identify pain.
We don't recognize and respect the fragility of life until we lose someone we love or almost completely lose ourselves.
We don't fully trust and seek God until we have exhausted all of our own efforts or learn the hard way that others can and will let us down.

Life is ironic, which is why we should be intentional.

Perhaps one of the most profound takeaways
about feeling you are hidden, misunderstood,
or that everyone is wrong about you is the power
in discovering and protecting the truths of who you truly are.

Though everyone preaches the importance of reputation,
at the end of the day, it is relative.

Your reputation and image are different in the mind of every
individual who crosses your path and can be influenced by
opinions, optics, and even another person's own insecurities.

Your character, however, is not who you appear to be.
It reflects who you truly are within.

I am putting unspoken, subconscious,
and deep-seeded wounds to rest.

I am pivoting from pain.
I'm finding myself grateful for all lessons.
I'm freeing myself from all shame and suffering.

I am fully forgiving myself and others.
Resentment and condemnation have no space
or authority in my mind, body, or spirit.

God did not give me a spirit of fear;
but, He did give me a testimony, a hope,
and a voice for me to boldly use.

That past pain and pressure still hurts deeply, not because you aren't healed or working on releasing it, but because you are attached to the version of yourself that experienced it.

Your discontentment is not a result of what you see but rather a result of what you refuse to let go of.

For you to truly move on, have peace, and walk in the boldness of who you were created to be, you must free yourself from the former things.

Allow the former version of you to rest in peace, so the current version of you can rise in purpose.

You have to let it go.

I know you mentally, spiritually, and emotionally held on to it for years because it changed you in ways the world will never truly understand or see. It permeated your soul and shifted your perspective on everything.

I acknowledge that holding on seemed like the safest and most natural action at the time and carrying your experiences also led you to many truths and realizations. However, that season of discovery and depression is over.

You have to develop from it all and also forgive the things you can't forget.

Fear cannot lead your next steps and the past is not allowed to follow you into your future.

It's time to release the former version of yourself and limitations you spoke over your journey, as you stand with the wisdom that was earned as you walk boldly into a new season of your life.

Holding on to every detail of the offense,
pain that was inflicted, or struggle you had
is not keeping you safe.
It is keeping you bound.

Dwelling on the suffering
is not creating an armor
from potential pain.
It is keeping it in.

I told myself I forgave
when I wasn't ready
then couldn't understand
why the resentment
and anger stayed in my mind
long after the words
of reconciliation
left my mouth.

Forgiveness is freedom, but its impact
is not truly experienced if it is not grounded
in sincerity, truth, and humility.

Give yourself permission to leave it all behind:
the pain, the humiliation, the suffering, and the struggles.

Give yourself permission to remove the shackles from your mind
as you step out of an internal prison created from shame, guilt,
and condemnation.

Give yourself permission to forgive yourself, and others, as you
acknowledge that we are all flawed people worthy of mercy,
grace, and restoration.

Give yourself permission.

I'm letting go because I'm tired of being dragged. I'm tired of carrying the memories, pains, and unmet expectations of the past into my present thoughts.

I'm tired of being angry with people who have no idea of their wrongs and frustrated with those who genuinely do not care. I'm tired of waiting for fairness when I know life is no fairy tale. I'm tired of struggling to move forward today because I suffered yesterday. I'm tired of replaying my regrets and punishing myself over the hurt I caused others, or that I allowed into my life.

I will let it go and every ounce of anger with it.

I will move forward with the wisdom life left me, without meditating on the needless worries and deep wounds that brought them. I will see the greater purpose behind every experience and emotion without meditating on the principles that kept me bound.

I'm free to acknowledge the hurt, free to recognize this impact without it becoming a present-day obstacle. I am free to finally let it go for good.

Your discontentment comes from
worrying about what people think
instead of standing on what you know.

You know better.
You know every detail of your conversations,
experiences, and emotions because they are yours alone.

You understand the background
of every optic and opinion
because you actually lived it.

Instead of dwelling on
the feelings and words of others,
rest in the truth and the fact
that you know better.

People projecting and portraying you
as whoever they want to see you as is their choice.

You wasting your time, energy, and efforts
to convince them otherwise is your choice.

I'm not correcting, confirming, or clearing up anything.
I'm not giving a side especially if one isn't asked for because,
let's be honest, you're hell-bent on believing you're right
anyway.

I'm no longer shrinking my energy and essence in your presence
because you choose not to see me as the person I am.

Your insults, insinuations, and audacity – I will not offer a single
reaction to. At most, I will speak life over you.

Believe, say, and think what you want.
The fruit of my life will shed more light
on my character than any falsehoods
or shade you throw.

Forgive others no matter if they ask for it,
or have changed as you choose to release
the part of you that can't undo what was done
and you hold firmly to the lessons you learned.

A person misunderstanding or misinterpreting your experience or emotions does not change a single aspect of your reality.

It simply changes how another person perceives or views your reality.

In order to make room
for your blessings and breakthrough,
you must release the weight of burdens
and clear your environment of what brings you down.

When I needed love,
you gave me lessons.

When I needed a friend, you taught me the importance of being my own.

I proved myself to you through my loyalty, patterns, and support long before we came to this point. I fiercely protected you and consistently stood by you. But, when I needed you most, I had to protect myself from you.

I expected so much more; yet, found myself making terms with the fact that though my efforts were not for nothing. In the end, I would get nothing in return.

All those unmet expectations and assumptions did was leave me angry, anxious, and alone. Upset that you didn't reciprocate what I so genuinely gave; yet, accepting that you couldn't give what you didn't have.

It wasn't your fault for letting me down. It was my fault for receiving revelation long before but refusing to turn you loose. Before you betrayed me, I betrayed myself.

When all was said and done, I learned from you. I learned how I never wanted to make any person I love feel, and I learned to identify patterns and people that were not aligned with my life. I now see blessings where I once saw bitterness and learned to detach from what is draining me – not out of hate but out of self-love.

Most importantly, I learned to see you as a teacher and never an enemy. You taught the importance of discernment, the power of saying less than needed, and how to truly forgive what you likely won't forget.

I am not mad at you,
I'm grateful for you.
Grateful for the good times
that made me smile
and the bad times
that made me wiser.

Grieving those whose hearts are still beating
yields pain that most people experience
yet few are willing to express.

People will disrespect you, degrade you,
and seemingly do everything in their power
to aid in devaluing in you.

Then, they will be perplexed when your response
isn't reciprocated disrespect – it is distance.

When everything in you wants to go off, get out of character, or put another person in their place, remember the strength and wisdom that come from respecting revelation.

Keep calm, keep your peace, and move in love as you wisely move forward.

Perhaps the reason they didn't give you compassion, understanding, and respect is because those are qualities they do not possess within themselves.

It was not because they hated you, wanted to hurt you, or found joy in your pain.

So often, our first reaction is to take offense and exude anger, but we must be mindful that our expectation of how a person will treat us should be in alignment with what they've shown us, not merely what we've shown them or what we believe we deserve.

A person cannot give you something they don't have, no matter how many times you've given it to them.

Trust people to be who they are.
Trust them to love you or leave you.
Trust them to support you or separate from you.
Trust them to live their life freely as you live yours.

No matter how much you love someone,
desire reciprocation, or feel that your views are best,
you do not have ownership, full influence, or control
over anyone but yourself.

Praying for your enemy seems unfathomable
until you realize you are your own worst enemy.

When you begin to accept that the person who has spoken the
most doubt, fear, and confusion over your life is the person in the
mirror and the one who will lead you to replay every pain of the
past in your present is in your mind—you embrace the truth that
resentment towards people, though valid and burdensome, is
nothing compared to the impact of regretting the flaws, failures,
and foolishness of the person you once were.

There is pain in looking back and seeing your part in your pain,
how your choices impacted others, or how you could have better
handled situations, struggles, and suffering. There is power and
freedom in forgiving, releasing, and healing oneself.

To move forward, you must forgive the person who let you down
most and the person you've condemned and questioned all along.

You must forgive yourself.

It's okay to let it thicken your skin,
but do not allow it to harden your heart.

It's okay to let it shift and mature your perspective,
but do not allow it to puncture your spirit
and rob you of your personality.

I was angry and resentful
because you didn't understand me.
You didn't see me.

You didn't believe the truth
I was sharing with you
and didn't provide protection
and support in a time I needed it most.

No matter how much my spirit holds no hatred
and my heart wants to be around,
my body won't allow me to.

It's as if I'm frozen in survival mode
when around people I've had to heal from
questioning every word that leaves my lips.

Not because I don't care for them,
but because they've taught me
I can't be vulnerable around them.

In the end, I realized
the hurt never turned to hate.
No matter how much my emotions
led me to feel so.
I never stopped loving people.

I stopped trusting them.

What do you get out of hurting me or seeing me hurt?
Please help me understand.

How does knowing that I'm shaken, stressed, and struggling help
you in any way? How can anyone putting me down equate to
you feeling as though you are being built up?

I've tried to put myself in your shoes, see it through your level of
perception, and imagine how treating someone in a way you
know they'd never treat you could yield a positive response.

But I couldn't.

There is no way I could see someone I love or value hurting and
seeing their pain wouldn't hurt me. And if I in any way
contributed to that, there is no way I'd be without remorse or
conviction.

There is no way I could sit back and know someone I care about
is crying while I sit there and laugh at them. I can't see it, which
is why I no longer have the desire to see you.

I don't believe I could ever hate anyone I've genuinely loved – family or friend. I could not attack anyone I've ever gone out of my way to protect.

No matter what factors and emotions are involved or if my ego gets bruised and my heart gets broken in the process. My love for them is still there underneath it all. For me, it was never transactional; it was always unconditional. Whether they realized and appreciated that fact or not.

It doesn't matter what they do or say, how much they hurt me, or if their actions show they don't see, value, or love me to the extent I do for them. I won't argue, prove myself, or get out of character. I'll just get out of the way. It's not that I don't find them worthy enough to fight for. It is because I accept the difference between fighting for the bonds and people you love, as well as understanding and accepting when they are willingly fighting against you.

Even if they break me into pieces, I know it will hurt me more if I shatter them in any way because I don't want to hurt them.

So, I've learned to love people from a distance and speak life over them, even if I know that energy is not reciprocated towards me, or my separation is not understood.

Discernment taught me and continues to reveal that those hurting you are only hurt people within themselves. When the time comes that they want to heal from within, I don't want any harsh or hurtful words I once spoke to lead them to think I won't be a safe space to help or support their healing.

Sometimes you must silence the flesh's desire
to focus on the principle of the matter
and remember that everything is spiritually
connected and has a greater purpose.

All this time, I thought the heaviness and discomfort I had towards you was unforgiveness.

The type of heaviness that makes you think about a person or a situation and completely get immersed in the offense or disdain as if it just happened.

As time passed and my healed eyes opened, I realized it wasn't unforgiveness or merely my inability to forget.

It was grief.

I was mourning the person I thought you were, the bond I thought we had, and the future I always pictured you in.

I was grieving because I was accepting that your seasons in my life had expired.

Give yourself time and compassion to grieve
the loss of what you wanted or had
but also have hope for what remains
and what will be.

I do not hold grudges
but life has taught me the importance
of clinging to boundaries.

MORGAN RICHARD OLIVIER

One of the most impactful and life changing acts of love you can extend to yourself is replacing condemnation with compassion and exchanging resentment with reframing.

For many of us, we struggle with forgiving others, moving forward from difficult seasons, and often dangle our struggles with the truth that life is a journey – an imperfect one at that.

We will have seasons of consecutive wins but those seasons are often followed by seasons of life-altering losses. There will be times where we make situations exponentially worse by trying to fix them and other times where it will seem everything we touch turns to gold. There will be family and friends we would do anything in our power to protect, who will be the exact individuals we will find ourselves mentally, spiritually, and emotionally protecting ourselves from.

No matter the season or how it appears, how we choose to reframe and redirect from life's hills and valleys will not only impact our destination but also the timing and levels of peace we experience while venturing there.

137

There is healing in letting go
of anger and offense.
There is healing in understanding
that not everyone thinks
and has the same heart you do.

You can't control anyone.
You can only control yourself
and remind yourself that others
are worthy of the compassion, mercy,
and forgiveness you pray for.

How long do I need to ponder
on the fact that you hurt me
before I accept the fact
that you are a hurt person, too?

the freedom of forward

It's amazing how pain and pride influences a person.

I refused to forgive and pray for you
because I didn't feel you deserved it.
I was ignorant to the truth
that doing so would set me free as well.

I was angry, hurt, and crippled by the wound
while I was also self-loathing, dwelling, and accepting
the part I played in it.

Truth is we are all different, imperfect people
seeing through our vastly different worldviews
and making decisions we think are best at the time.

Whether right or wrong, weak or wise,
no words spoken, action carried out, or day lived
can be redone, revised, or removed from the past.

Therefore, choose to reframe it,
learn to respect the revelations, and respect
that redirection came with the lessons you've acquired.

There are some breaks in your heart
an apology or acknowledgement
could never piece back together.

There are some scars so deep
sitting down with the person
who cut you could not soothe them.

No matter if words are exchanged
or points are proven, you must accept
that closure never comes
from anyone who hurt you.

It comes from healing within yourself
and not allowing what you experienced
in the past to make you bitter today
or fearful of the future.

I realized that I never hated anyone in my life.

Yes, there were times I was offended by people who made a point to hurt me or distract me, but their sting never impacted me like the offenses I received from those I considered myself close to.

The feeling of having people in your face yet learning they don't have your back or best interests at heart is difficult to accept. It's even more difficult to release because that realization not only makes you question if you can trust others, it also makes you question if you can trust your own judgment.

The anger, resentment, and disdain that stemmed from being disregarded, disrespected, or disappointed by those I truly deeply and genuinely loved.

It wasn't hatred.
It was unexpected hurt.

Some people are hard to forgive because you never expected
the pain they so easily, cunningly, and gladly served you
to impact your life, mindset, and personality to the extent
it did.

Without that person exhibiting an ounce of remorse or
conviction, you felt it was unfair they could continue enjoying
their life while knowing the efforts they made to hurt you and
needless attacks you endured left you in pieces and unable to
process.

No matter what they did or said, you must accept the truth that
keeping them bound with unforgiveness will only keep you
bound and unable to move forward.

Forgive them, even if they never apologize or make an initiative
to right what they know was always wrong.

Forgive them, even if those wounds cut to the depth of your soul.

Forgive them, because it's time for you to fully be free.

I spent years being angry.
Blaming you for taking my power.
Condemning myself for being in
in a position to be hurt.
Resenting all you did and didn't do.

The truth is you never took anything.
I gave it to you.

I gave you my power
because I gave you access to
my energy, attention, and emotions.

You won't always know why, and you also won't need to.

As a person who searches yourself and wants to understand the source of your choices and reactions, it's natural that you want to understand the actions and reactions of others – especially those who made a lasting impression on you.

Maybe understanding their hurt would make the pain they inflicted upon you more tolerable. Perhaps gaining an understanding of their worldview, path, or mindset would reveal how they do not see what you perceive as an error in their ways. Possibly discovering a rational reason for the situation or behavior would make it easier for you to put it behind you.

What you must realize is, obtaining that information will not undo what is done or how it affected you.

Even if you can't uncover the root of your issue, you can reframe it. Focus on what you can control within yourself. Remember, you don't need an apology in order to gain closure. Allow yourself to feel, express, process, and release it all.

None of that requires another person's permission or input. Heal from what hurt you.

Pray for them because for anyone to have the ability
to create such chaos, division, and confusion in your life,
you know those strongholds already reside within them.

Pray they experience the type of healing that not only changes
their mind, but completely changes their life.

Pray they discover the power of faith so deeply, any void or
vicious cycles they find themselves overwhelmed by can be
overcome and filled with love, peace, and conviction that only an
encounter with God can provide.

When the people you loved and protected
turn into life lessons and wisdom from wounds,
you begin to accept that no one and nothing in life
is in your control.

All you can do is apply the insight you've acquired
and use it to mature and better discern.

Everyone who hurts you is supposed to.
Everyone that lies to you or about you is supposed to.
Everyone who uses you, takes advantage of your vulnerability,
or leads you to unnecessary pain as supposed to.

Not because it is right.
Not because it is anywhere close to being fair.
Not because you're suffering is without regard.

Because it quickens you.
Because it humbles you.
Because it aligns you with who you were created to become.

There are some storms you must endure so God can fully trust
you and confidently use you in seasons. Chapters of your life
you must battle in silence but boldly talk about as testimonies
after you overcome.

Nothing in life is merely about *me*.
It's always mentally, spiritually, and emotionally about *we*.

It's about not only learning and applying your life lessons but
also having the discernment and understanding, eager to
maturely pass that wisdom on to someone else who needs it.

There are some pains
you must navigate needlessly
so you know how to handle yourself
in similar situations and have
the empathy to extend to others in the future.

Thank you for rejecting me.
Thank you for not hearing or believing me.
Thank you for showing me who you are
because all that pain led me to fully healing
and discovering who I am.

You taught me true power is not shown
by having people stand up for you or stand with you.
True strength shines when a person can face themselves
and stand on their own.

MORGAN RICHARD OLIVIER

A genuine conversation needs to be had,
eyes need to be looked into,
energy needs to be felt,
and intentions need to be made known.

The presence of confusion stems
from the lack of clarity.

If everything can't be clearly,
credibly, and confidentially
laid out on the table,
don't waste your time sitting at it.

You can be friendly to a person you've forgiven,
yet still not trust them or want to be their friend.

You can speak life into them, pray for them, and bless them from
the depths of your heart without reserving a place in your life,
circle, or future for them.

Apologies do not mean
that person automatically returns
to having full access to you.

Reconciliation does not mean
you ever desire for them to regain
the role they once had.

No matter what has happened,
how far we've drifted apart,
or what led us to detach...

If I wanted the best for you then,
I want the best for you now.

No matter what words we exchanged,
how much we disappointed each other,
or how much pain sprang forth...

If I prayed for you then,
I pray for you now.

Because no matter if our bond expired,
how deeply our feelings were hurt,
or if your chapter in my book of life has ended...

If I loved you then,
I love you now.

The one who defames your character detoxes your circle. The one who manipulates you exposes your strengths and weaknesses.

As much as I held resentment and rage towards people in my life, there was one positive trait every person who intentionally hurt me had in common – they taught me.

They taught me the importance of accountability, self-assessment, inner work, and seeking God for instruction. They revealed every person who had a gift of smiling in my face and stabbing me in my back. They helped reveal my own immaturity, unrealistic expectations I have for myself and others, and the importance of discernment.

They introduced me to a version of myself I never should have been which, in turn, led me to develop and discover the person I was created to be.

Therefore, those who've hurt me, used me, or disrespected me are not my enemies, opposition, or concern. They are my teachers, challengers, and catalysts for creativity and conviction. Their madness is my muse.

You didn't destroy my life. You detoxed it.

For years, I felt the extent of my struggles, suffering, and silence was unspoken, needless, and overlooked. After the tears dried and clarity came, I found solace in the fact that each step of my journey revealed lessons, wisdom, and understanding that no book, conversation, or observation could have ever taught me.

I had to live it, fight it, and overcome it to truly bloom into the person that I am. I had to uproot my routines, mindset, and expectations to not only gain an awareness of the person I am but also to acquire the confidence needed to walk in my power – even when that meant I was walking alone.

I had to accept that you would only be as powerful, impactful, and relevant in my life as my energy, insecurity, and innermost thoughts allowed you to be. And you never deserved the amount I gave.

So, here I stand and stop.

At this very moment, I take it all back – every ounce of freedom, focus, and feeling I once gave you as I give myself the permission, security, and love to move forward and leave you behind.

I forgave you for hurting me
but I didn't forgive myself
for putting myself in a position
to be hurt by you.

It was beyond taking accountability
for my own failures, foolishness, or faults.
It was condemning, self-loathing, and
punishing to myself because I should have
known or done better.

By dwelling on my choices and the truth that
the signs were there but my discernment was not,
I fully excused your inexcusable efforts and outcomes
as I picked up a level of shame, silence, and scrutiny
that was never mine to hold.

Carrying criticism, chaos, and consequences
that were never earned yet never expressed.

I let you off the hook
as I impaled myself.

Being let down by others
is unfortunate yet expected.
Letting yourself down yields
a pain that is immeasurable,
yet feels impossible to release.

Of all the people and pains I've ever struggled to release, the one who has been undoubtedly the hardest to forgive is myself.

Forgiving myself for my reactions, actions, and ignorance of the past has been a feat with crippling, complex layers attached to it.

At times, it seemed easier to hold on to the wounds than allowing them to heal. Maybe it is because I should have known better. Maybe it is because I wish I knew then what I know now. Maybe it is because my unmet expectations and unexpressed offenses created a battlefield within my mind that it felt like time, healing, therapy, praying, and positivity could not overthrow.

Whatever the root of that reason may have been, the fruit it bore was condemnation, shame, and relentless ruminating thoughts. Thoughts that made me question my worth and question my life. Thoughts that made me so fearful to trust others that I didn't allow the right people in.

Trauma that not only shifted my mindset and personality but also the view of myself and the world around me.

Why is it easier to forgive
the person standing before you
than it is to forgive the person
struggling within you?

Forgive the person you once were
so you can embrace the freedom
of loving and accepting the person
you are now.

I'm not the good guy in everyone's story.
I've been the villain, the fool, and the lesson.

And as much as I've addressed myself, repented, and learned to
apply my lessons, I would be lying if I said I didn't look back
occasionally and criticize the seasons that broke my heart and
opened my eyes.

I believe the unspoken dark side of gaining wisdom and maturity
is the ability to easily shine light on all the ways you could have
done better or been better.

It's realizing that what you thought was the best course of action
in one season only created more hurt to heal from in another.

Accepting the truth that you have been the reason behind another
person's tears because you have hurt others both knowingly and
unknowingly.

Forgiving myself was always a more difficult task than forgiving others because the lines between condemnation and conviction always seem to be skewed.

I gave everyone else permission and excuses to be human, make mistakes, or make wrong decisions; but, I held myself to a caliber and expectation that was not healthy or attainable.

Whether I harped on old issues with fresh eyes, struggled to release regret, or replay the parts I played in the pains I experienced like a broken record – I carried weights of shame, anger, insecurity, resentment, and fear to the point where it *made more sense* to focus on my faults than to release them.

Forgive yourself.
Deep down inside you know
it is long overdue.

There is nothing you can do to change the outcome of what
happened, undo the words spoken and left unsaid, or take away
the tears that came from feeling like so much was taken from
you.

But, you can forgive.

You can acknowledge the lessons, apply them, and be grateful,
for it all led to this version of you.

You can extend the love, mercy, and grace you extend to others
as you remember the person you're seeking to forgive is the
former version of yourself.

It is okay to not be proud of that pain or readily willing to talk
about it, but it is time to remove it from your shoulders, release it
from your mind, and lay it in God's hands once and for all.

He has forgiven you,
forgotten about it,
and used it for your good.

Now, it is time you do the same.

I wish I could have helped you,
helped you process and navigate it all.
You went from feeling on top of the world
to feeling like you'd never been so small.

Every emotion, so unfamiliar
and unbearable at the time,
left you numb and unable
to trust yourself or others…no matter if
their intentions were pure or kind.

Your mind was on fire
and so was your life.
From having a heart of hope
to it being ridden with strife,

With so much to say,
your lips never moved.
Your silent tears taught you
when your points were not proved.

Have solace in the fact
that each trial and triumph was worth it.
You may have lost your way
but you ultimately found your purpose.

It's amazing how as we grow, heal, and mature we sometimes find ourselves remembering the days before our faith was our focus, our mindsets were renewed, and our lives were in order.

Many of us slip into condemnation, shame, and guilt as we recall those *if I knew then what I know now* experiences.

We wouldn't have made that choice, spoken those words, or handled that situation in that way, but we did. We wouldn't have allowed our emotions to impact our logic, let the pains within our hearts create pains in other people's lives, or accepted malicious treatment from others for that long, but we did.

No matter what the case may be, we must remind ourselves we are human, we don't always make the right decisions, hindsight is 20/20, and everyone has a chapter they don't want to read out loud.

You've been chastised and changed,
condemnation is not your portion.

I know you wish you knew then what you know now. I know if
you could go back in time, you'd handle it all differently. I know
the page they refer to is not nearly a representation of the book
of your life you lived...but, it's over.

There are no redos or revisions. There are only revelations
gained from your experiences and the need for you redirect and
apply those lessons you've learned.

Forgive your former self.

That version of you handled it all the best way you thought you
could at the time. Since then, you've worked tirelessly to do and
be better. Extend to yourself the love, grace, forgiveness, and
mercy you extend to everyone else.

The past version of yourself
deserves forgiveness
and the present version of yourself
deserves peace.

When your what ifs turn into even ifs,
you will know that the tide has turned
and spiritually, you have shifted.

When you find peace in surrendering
and serenity in putting all
that you once carried down,
you will rest in the fact that faith
blooms where fear once burdened.

You can continue to cry over the pains of the past that broke
your heart yet opened your eyes, call yourself every name in the
book, and recall every detail you experienced throughout your
life.

Or maybe, just maybe
you can use the wisdom and knowledge
you acquired from it all to honestly look
a person in their eyes and genuinely say
I've been there.

Maybe you can tell yourself,
But I know better now.

Maybe you can finally
extend the grace and compassion
you denied yourself for so long by saying
I forgive you.

You were never expected to regain bonds that broke you or return full access to those who abused it. You were simply supposed to forgive what happened, forgive yourself, and embrace the freedom of doing so.

You were never required to share your trauma, trials, or troubles with everyone or expected to hold yourself captive from your shortcomings. You were only responsible for uprooting and understanding what held you bound, treating your ails and issues, and healing your heart from the inside out.

You were never strong enough to carry the weights of regret, resentment, and ridicule. You were always meant to give it to God and allow Him to be your strength as you embrace the restorative beauty of redemption, repentance, and redirection.

You are tired, not because you are out of faith or out of God's view but because you are out of order mentally, spiritually, and emotionally, and overstepping in areas where revelation showed you to stop.

You ruminate because you can clearly recognize the violation. Replaying scenarios aimlessly to solve a past problem will only lead to create a mental problem in the present.

Understand that you can mentally fixate on a hard time all day, but it will never fix what happened yesterday.

Instead of allowing your regrets, unresolved issues, and resentments to lead you to question your worth and identity, learn to reframe how you look at it and create a new viewpoint that further affirms something positive sprang from the experience.

In doing so, you not only begin to recognize the positive and powerful impact a once painful, pressure-filled experience created but also revel in the truth it gave you the endurance and insight you needed to be the impactful and enlightened person you are now.

There are tears that taught us,
suffering that strengthened us,
and wounds that shaped our wisdom.

If there's one truth we've grown to be grateful for, it's that all
things work together. Whether you initially pass or fail tests and
trials, there is a lesson to be learned and countless opportunities
to apply them.

Look back, not with regret or resentment but with respect as you
appreciate your resilience and ability to redirect every piece of
the past which served as a necessary steppingstone that prepared
you.

You can say it paid off.

You gained a greater perspective, learned countless lessons, and found joy on this journey of fully discovering who you are and to whom you belong.

But it cost you.

It cost you your immaturity, ignorance, and excuses. It cost you unequally yoked bonds, toxic mindsets, and environments that you would later outgrow.

It cost your naive view of reality, perfectionism, and the life plan you had.

You had to lose to gain.
Thankfully, you've grown to accept
everything you lost,
you don't ever want back.

MORGAN RICHARD OLIVIER

The slate is wiped clean.
I forgive the past and the pains that came with it.

Whether those scars were once cuts from the consequences of
my own actions and reactions, or were the results of chaos that
came from someone else's efforts – I wash my hands of it all as I
willingly turn away.

The past is not my place of residence or a mind frame I should
revisit more than I revel in the present.

It happened. I learned. I let go.

With one finger and one moment at a time, I'm mentally spiritually, and emotionally releasing my grasp of the burdens I carried in my head or heart.

I relinquish every ounce of the control I once thought I had and embrace the beauty of having faith and following the path destined for me.

There is nothing behind me that didn't prepare me for what's ahead. There are no tears that crossed my face that didn't open my eyes and teach me all I needed to learn.

With one foot in front of the other and my head held high, I will finally leave the former things behind and arrive as the person I know I am.

I will see and be seen.
I will rise and reach higher heights.

An exercise from your healed self to your hurt self:

Take a deep breath and close your eyes.
I want you to think back to the weakest, lowest, and most vulnerable version of yourself.

I want you to envision your exact location, make note of your physical features, and even remember the smells around you. I want you to tap into the emotions that laid in your heart, the thoughts that ran through your mind, and recall the waves of obstacles you once endured.

Then, I want you to look that former version of yourself softly in the eyes and tell them, "*I see you.*"

Hug your past self and tell yourself, "*I feel you.*"

Hold the hands of the person you once were and say, "*I forgive you.*"

Speak life to a version of yourself that felt it was drifting away and stand as proof that there is healing, hope, and wholeness on the other side of this season if they keep holding on.

175

There is no song sweeter to hear
than the sound of your feet walking away
from what no longer serves you.

Letting go is realizing
that holding on was only
holding you back.

the freedom of forward

PART III: FORWARD

A butterfly in a jar, though admired
by those who cross its path, can never be
fully appreciated or reach the heights
it's intended to until it is released.

At some point,
you will grow tired
of fighting yourself
and you will begin to fight
for everything you deserve.

There is nothing more beautiful and empowering than watching a person finally choose themselves and fully embrace the magnitude of who they are.

Refined by fire and unfazed by external validation or internal insecurity, they awaken from their ashes and rise as their authentic selves.

MORGAN RICHARD OLIVIER

The pain was used to pivot me to my purpose.
The destruction, discomfort, and darkness was used
to get me to my development, discernment, and destination.

As much as it hurt me and led me to question every aspect of
myself and my path, it also led me to shift my perspective as I
gained a greater respect and understanding of the healing
process.

Some of the most beautiful pearls of wisdom can only be created
through the pressure that comes with crippling experiences,
unwavering faith, and what seems to be an existential crisis.

Therefore, I will allow them to be what they are – life lessons
and the opportunities to grow mentally, spiritually, and
emotionally. I will extend grace, love, and forgiveness to myself
and release the chokehold that shame, fear, and guilt had on me
for so long.

I give myself permission to live in peace.
I give myself permission to detach from what drains me.
I give myself permission to show up as my authentic self.
I give myself permission to forgive others and myself.
I give myself permission to thrive.

You were built for this.

Every single lesson you learned and applied,
pruned and prepared you for this moment.

You owe it to yourself to bring this to fruition.
You owe it to your healed self to thrive.

When you think back about all the pain and suffering you experienced, make a point to also reflect on all that God didn't allow to come to you.

Think about all the evil you encountered that God turned around for your good. The weapons that came but didn't prosper. Think of the wounds He used for you to gain wisdom and ultimately walk in your purpose.

He allowed you to experience it all but didn't allow anything to overtake you, and that is a blessing you should always be far more grateful for.

Sometimes it's easy to forget all the good you've done,
the good you've experienced and the goodness within you
because what you perceive as bad always stands out the most for
you. Instead of viewing it as a burden in your life, see the
blessing that was always standing behind it.

You needed adversity, competition, failure, and struggle to truly
learn, mature, evolve, and gain wisdom. What felt like breaking
and bruising was building you the entire time.

Therefore, view it all as steppingstones that aligned you with
self-discovery, bolstered your faith, and equipped you with
empathy on this beautiful journey called life.

A journey that is not only teaching and enriching you, but also
inspiring and enlightening others.

There are some emotions and situations you must fully experience to truly understand. No matter your heart posture and the amount of compassion and kindness extended, it will never compare to the words from a person who lived it.

There is an unspoken language and unprecedented empathy that comes with connecting with someone who has faced the same mountain as you.

The emotions, thoughts, and impact their valleys impressed upon them are unique. The wisdom they gained, used to testify from the hills, undeniable.

That is why learning your lessons, sharing your testimony, and becoming the type of person you needed at your darkest times is imperative.

In a world where everyone judges, assumes, and condemns, you have the influence to empower, educate, and encourage. You didn't overcome your obstacles for yourself alone.

Let your life's journey be the map that leads another person to their road of inner freedom.

There will come a time in your life where you will realize that you do not have all the answers, you have limitations of control, and some of your efforts do not always equal the outcome of your desire.

When you begin to see life is less about perfection and performance and more about perspective and purpose, you will gain the key that unlocks the beautiful gift of peace.

There is power in being present, finding gratitude in the blessings you have and the burdens you don't, and simply breathing as each moment passes.

the freedom of forward

My spirit is at peace
and my heart is now whole
as I look back at my life and embrace
that everything I experienced
is well with my soul.

I lay my burdens down
with every offense I've forgiven
yet struggled to forget,
and accept the truth that all I've learned
is connected to the version of myself
I have not yet met.

There is truly nothing but peace,
love, and clarity left in my heart at this point.

No blame, no contempt, and no heaviness.

I'm simply grateful for each lesson,
living each day to the fullest,
and keeping my faith in focus.

There is beauty in looking back and seeing old pressures with a new perspective. From my emotions and experiences, to the ways I held on and times I held myself back – I not only understand the motives behind my movements but clearly see the divine strategy and impact of obedience and restraint.

It was undoubtedly my faith and trust in God that not only brought me through the darkest times but also healed me through them. Seasons where I didn't utter a word but confirmation and revelation about myself and those around me spoke volumes.

Therefore, I accept the reality that what felt like destruction was truly development. Everything that appeared to be falling apart was actually coming together and ended up working together for my good.

Everyone is silently carrying a cross you know nothing about, a burden their loved ones are blind to, and an emotional void that goes without being voiced.

Although you can't simply take their pains, pressures, and problems away – your words, actions, and reactions can either add a layer to them or lighten the load.

Smile at strangers, be kind to those who cross your path, and extend grace at the frequency you would like to receive it.

We are all humans doing our best, trying to find our way, and learning every single day.

Lead with love and compassion as you not only embody the type of person you once needed but also become the change the world needs to see.

I'm grateful for the people who never left.

The people who protected and loved me both
in front of my face and behind my back.
The people who believed me and believed in me,
even when it felt like the world chose not to.

The people who prayed for me when
I couldn't find the faith and lifted me up
when I didn't have the strength.
The people who celebrate my successes,
push me to my fullest potential,
and are a proven safe space.

I'm grateful for those whose love
was proven by their actions
and reinforced with their words.

I love you and appreciate you
more than you'll ever know.

I appreciate those who adjusted my crown
without telling the world how heavy it had become
and spoke life to me when I couldn't
utter an encouraging word.

I'm grateful that I consistently cross paths with people who
recognize the power and potential in others and take it upon
themselves to congratulate, compliment, and collaborate – yet
never try to compare, crush, or compete.

I value individuals who authentically spread kindness,
compassion, and wisdom everywhere they go and leave people
better than they found them.

I love when a person can love others and influence them to do
the same.

There is power in being a good person and an impact that
reaches far beyond that initial interaction.

Be someone who reminds others that there are genuine people in
the world and inspires them to be great.

Be the person you needed, yet may have never had.
Be the one who shows others the freedom of truth
by simply being yourself.

Some people do not look like
what they've been through
because they never went through
what you said about them.

MORGAN RICHARD OLIVIER

Much of your insecurity stems
from striving to please and prove yourself
to people instead of embracing and accepting
the powerful truth of who you are.
Placing outside validation on a pedestal
that only God's views and love of you should have.

I believe you.

Even if no one else does.
Even if the optics and emotions are against you, and it feels like everyone else is, too. If the lies you are hearing make you question the truths within you – know that I believe you.

I see you.

Even if it feels you are hidden in plain sight.
Even if you feel invisible to the ones around you. If you feel misunderstood by the ones who should know you best, unappreciated by those you've done the most for, or viewed through the lens of other people's projections – know that I see you.

When you feel unseen, unheard, or unbelieved, know that there are people who can see, feel, and hear you from a mile away. There are people who will protect and preserve you both in front of your face and behind your back. People whose love for you will forever outweigh any hatred you receive. Most importantly, there is a person who sees and knows you clearly. And that person is you.

Do not allow the words and ways of others to impact how you speak to, support, or view yourself. See, know, and respect who you are, and you will align with others who will do the same.

The truth does not expire,
no matter how long ago you lived it.

Whether you share it at the time
or many years later, it will forever be
your story to tell.

Have you ever considered the possibility
that it isn't a matter of people not seeing
who you are, knowing the truth,
or appreciating your light?

Rather, it is the bias in them that makes it easier
not to acknowledge the goodness in you?

Normalize allowing people to keep
whatever image or opinion
they have towards you
without feeling the need
to correct them or prove yourself.

Sometimes all you need to do is live...
without proving, posting, or putting yourself
in a position to have your peace jeopardized.

Just walk in truth, work on yourself,
and fully embrace who you are.

You do not have to say a word.
Your fruit will tell all.

I used to care about what people thought, wanted to please everyone, and put the world's comfort before mine. Now that I have grown, am continuing to heal, and have discovered the value of knowing myself, I have become more selective, less reactive, and mindful of what matters.

I want to be around people I love and who truly love me back, mind my business, and live in peace as I walk in my purpose.

I desire conversations with those who I don't have to second guess the words I speak because I know they are listening to understand and engage – not to project or insult.

I seek to sit across tables with individuals who see me as the person I am and encourage me to become the person I was created to be.

I laugh, dance, and sing with those who bring joy into my life and give a sense of security as I fully immerse in each moment I spend with them.

I make time to fellowship, create memories with, and confide in those I love, trust, and enjoy.

Release the guilt associated with letting go and moving forward.

It's time to stop holding yourself back
in hopes that the ones you love and always saw potential in
will catch up with you or waiting for them to show support
or be happy that you've evolved.

You must make peace with the fact
that your progress, pivot, and peace
will require you to leave that
former version of yourself, your fears,
and your limitations behind.

Shower yourself with love,
compassion, and grace
like there is no tomorrow.

Give yourself the hope you need
to leave the past behind.
Speak life over your future and envision
that version of yourself in detail.

I don't need to be everyone's favorite,
the most beautiful person in the room,
or live a life of perfection and performance.

I simply want to live in a way
that pleases God, utilizes my gifts,
and aligns me with the internal
and external love I was assigned
to send and receive.

Breathe.

Unclench your jaw, relax your shoulders, and just be.

You made it through everything you once believed would overtake you. You survived the longest nights and endured many excruciating pains.

But look at you. You made it. You survived it. You're here.

Allow yourself to be present in this moment as you focus within – feeling, being, and fully embracing the essence of all that you are.

You are safe to receive
and extend genuine love.
Not everyone is the person
or people who hurt you.

Align yourself with people who can reaffirm you
when you can't recognize yourself.

Those that pray for you when you don't have
the faith to press forward.

Individuals who can comfort you
when it feels you have nowhere to turn.
People who you feel safe to rest and release
around who have your best interest at heart.

Let Them Love You

You need to let people love you.
Let them support you.
Let them be the safe space that they are
as you share your truth, vulnerability,
and aspirations with them.
Let them encourage you to reach new heights
as they push you to pursue the passions and purpose
you've had all along.

In due time, you will realize not everyone
is like the person or people who hurt you,
and you will find peace in receiving the love,
loyalty, and care you so genuinely give.

I'm grateful for what once brought me grief,
recognize the blessings in all I once perceived as burdens,
and see the power of revelation that once blinded me with pain.
I appreciate every ugly season I had
because they left me with beautiful lessons.

I'm grateful for every failure and foolish decision
I made and every effort to fix the behavior.

I'm thankful for every situation that felt
there was no fixing until God made a way.

Every hurt humbled me,
every pressure led me to pray,
and every setback set me up for
an even better version of myself.

Your testimony is the key
that unlocks the shackles
of another person's shame
and suffering.

May you have the courage to speak the truth
and the character and confidence to validate yourself,
even if others don't receive it, respect it, or believe it.

Instead of people-pleasing
and aiming to prove yourself,
learn to love others and yourself.

Instead of fixating on
disrespect received from other people
or times you didn't practice what you preached,
learn to forgive.

You must reach an understanding
that true restraint, faith, and order
are shown in how you react.

MORGAN RICHARD OLIVIER

If you struggle with how people perceive you, what they say, or fear judgment from others – know that their feelings toward you will never change the facts of who you are.

Their thoughts of you will never override the truths of your experiences, emotions, and intentions.

Their opinions are just that – opinions.

Know, love, and embrace who you truly are.
No one can give or take that from you.

the freedom of forward

Your truth, reality, and testimony are not shaken
simply because they do not align
with another person's projections toward you,
the opinions and optics they use to construct
your image in their head,
or the hearsay they choose to hold you to.

You know your life.
You lived every moment of it,
put one foot in front of the other
as you moved through it,
and heard every word in your mind
before it left your lips.

You know who you are
even if others do not.

You know every choice you've made and every word you've spoken. You know the complexity of your experiences and the impact of every influence and emotion you've endured.

And as you sit there trying to understand how people do not recognize or respect the evolution that has taken place within you or around you, remember they are merely spectators or characters in your book of life.

You became the safe space that you needed.

You learned to make room for people's emotions, vulnerability, and shame all while giving them the empathy and insight they needed to process and push through them.

You use the darkness you experienced to shed light on the suffering most people encounter yet seldom express.

If God allows you to be front row
for someone's transformation
do not remind them of who they once were.

Support them, cheer for them, and love them.

They already know the depths they had to climb out of,
as well as the pain and perception that came from it.

Do not remind them of who they've been.
Remind them that their testimony has a purpose
and there is a person they are destined to become.

Exposure may bring awareness,
but experience yields insight.
Failure is inevitable; yet, far too often,
we overlook the truth that it is valuable.

Contrary to what your comfort zones want you to believe, you
learn best by failure. You learn by breaking, then having to take
the time, patience, and genuine effort to restore what, at one
point, appeared to be ruined.

Oftentimes the greatest wisdom is acquired because you sought
it only after you were the greatest fool.

When you think of trial and error, the dark chapters of your
story, or the seasons that it seemed nothing was going right,
remember that same crushing, chaos, and confusion was also
your catalyst.

As I share my testimony in safe spaces,
I feel better. I breathe lighter.
I catch myself releasing loud exhales
and find myself lowering my shoulders –
exiting survival mode and embracing serenity.

It's as if everything I kept inside
was always meant to be let out.

Weapons formed but they didn't prosper.
Struggles came but you didn't stop.
The waiting that worried you turned into wisdom
and all that was revealed at rock bottom
only prepared you for the top.

All that frustrated you
worked in your favor.
What once held you back
is out of the way.

You may have lost yourself for a few seasons
but you found God.
You are proof that He makes a way.

You are the curse breaker of your family, the glue sent to mend another person's brokenness, and the key refined to unlock someone's shackles. Most importantly, you are a genuinely virtuous person whose gift of love runs purely through every word you speak and effort you extend.

I pray that you focus on the facts of who you are, who you are called to be, and to whom you belong. Though your feelings are valid, remember feelings are fickle. They do not define you or your faith walk.

Casting down all imaginations, insecurities, and irrational fears. Learn to speak life, truth, and peace over all that is within you and connect it to you. You are being delivered and developed.

Focus on the lessons and continue to move in ordered steps as you obey all ordered stops. All things are not only sent and allowed for a reason, but they are also working together for your ultimate good. Surrender, show up, and allow God to demolish any mental, generational, spiritual, and emotional chains.

Press on.

Do not be surprised when
those who dragged you through the mud
try to pick your flowers when you bloom.

Greet them with a fragrance
only God's favor can emit
and a radiance that flows freely from faith.

The storms and darkness did not break you.
They were the exact elements needed
for your roots and resilience to grow.

When you are called to love the people who left you, enlighten the very ones who insult you, and help lead those who hurt you to healing, you must silence your flesh and strengthen your spirit.

And you will not get to that point until you are tested, pruned, and trusted.

Prepare yourself to lift up the very individuals who knocked you down. Do not lose sight of your assignment when the ones you pray for and speak life over plot against and speak down on you.

The calling on your life, your position in your bloodline, and even the attacks connected to your anointing will require a level of wisdom that can't be withered and a willingness to serve that pride can never be a part of.

Hold fast to your peace, discern when to be still,
and know that though the pain is great,
your purpose is far greater.

I suffered, sought, and stood.
I prayed, pruned, and progressed.

And after it seemed so much left or changed,
a unique strength blossomed and stayed.

Be at peace with all that has come
and all that has gone.
Be at peace with the person you are
and allow yourself the freedom
of being authentically so.
Be at peace as you accept
all that is within your realm of control
and calmly release what is not yours to influence.

More than a state of mind or goal to achieve, peace is a choice to
operate from within no matter what is going on around you and a
true reflection of your mindset, heart posture, and sense of self.

I know every weight comes from me
trying to move forward with what you
do not want me to carry.

Every insecurity stems from me
and not seeing myself the way you do.

Every fear comes from not being willing to
fully trust you in that area and every doubt
comes from overthinking what you don't even want
on my mind in the first place.

Therefore, I give it to you and ask you to take it
out of my hands and mind for the very last time.

Hoping that you not only remember the tears
that crossed my face but also use the eyes
that once cried them to see joy and
divine strategy from it all.

It's not what people say about you,
it's what God knows and says about you.

Your anointing is not predicated on man's approval.
Do not be apprehensive about walking in your purpose
because someone does not acknowledge or appreciate it.

Boldly be the voice and vessel He called you to be.

It's unfamiliar and uncomfortable to walk in
uncharted territory but make the first step anyway.

Discover a side of life and yourself
you've yet to explore.

Seek to better understand the person within yourself
as you learn more about those around you.

There is no one prouder of you
than the person you once were.

The person who struggled
to speak their truth and protect their peace.

The person who so badly wanted the love
of others that they neglected to show love to themselves.

The person who saw the good in everyone else
yet couldn't identify, appreciate, and act upon
the goodness that always resided within them.

They are rooting for you, because unlike everyone else on this
earth, they know the extent of what you felt, all you overcame,
and all you had to lose to gain the wisdom, empathy, and
awareness you have now.

Your storm is over.
It is time for you to rest
and revel in the beauty it left behind.

You do not have to live in survival mode.
You do not have to hold yourself back or question your place.
You do not have to replay your issues or recall what happened.
You do not have to worry about what's coming next.

You endured, you learned, and you made it to the other side.

Now, instead of fixating
on what's behind,
look forward with faith.

You have been refined
and refreshed with a resilience
that cannot be denied.

Be the reason others
pursue redirection and believe
in the power of restoration.

Allow the good in you to reassure others
as they seek, reveal, and respect
the good within themselves.

You are walking in prayers you once prayed, dancing over living testimonies that once brought you to depression, and singing of the wisdom you gained through former struggles.

Now, do you see that every piece of your life both lived and imagined played a purpose?

Those dreams of yesterday you'll be living tomorrow, but first you must keep going. Ignore every distraction and all that wants to drain you. Dismantle any thought that holds your creativity and true capabilities captive. You owe it to yourself to bring this to fruition. Move forward.

You already have what it takes
to move forward and thrive.

Step into the unknown and unleash
the authority and impact within you.

There is a reason your comfort zone
now lacks contentment and your hopes
for the future seem more achievable.

Everything you need is already within you.

You are the only person who knows every version of you.

You are the only person who has lived your life, has seen everything through your eyes, has felt your emotions, and has had all your experiences from the beginning to now.

If you know every piece of the puzzle, every action, reaction, and emotion behind it, do not concern yourself about the opinions or optics of those who have not.

There is nothing people can tell you about yourself that you don't know. No one's opinions of you or feelings towards you can change the facts of who you are.

You have always been free,
but now you truly feel it.
Now, you truly see it in every
aspect of your life.

You have always had the choice
to move forward, but now
you have the confidence
and clarity to take those steps.

May you always remember how liberating
and lifechanging it was to let go and how impactful
and empowering the decision to dive deeper
within yourself, faith, and purpose was for you.

In this life, you will find yourself in situations
where you must take accountability
and rediscover the power that only truly forgiving
yourself and forgiving others can bring.

Give it to God, give yourself grace,
and give yourself permission
to do and be better through it all.

You are the reason I refuse to give up.
You are the reason I have the faith I have now.
You are the reason I hear the volume behind
a stranger's silence and learned to use my own voice.

I couldn't be who I am now without loving and learning
from who you were.

You – using everything that was broken, bruised, and buried
within you – taught me the importance of building with every
shattered piece and not throwing a single fragment or insight
away.

You, *the former version of myself,* needed to fall so
I could learn how to fly.

I see you.
I understand you.
I love you.
But now, I release you
and every fear, offense, and insecurity
that I carried with your memory.

Your impact and experiences will always be a part of the
chapters we shared. Now, it is time to continue writing my story
with your wisdom and without the weight of your wounds.

MORGAN RICHARD OLIVIER

Acknowledgments

To the person who has welcomed my words,
I thank you for not only embracing my journey
but also embarking on your own.

I thank you for meeting my experiences with empathy
and accepting my lessons with love.

May you never forget that healing, happiness, and wholeness
are not found by running to the outside world.
They are developed by returning to the stillness within
your most authentic self.

About the Author

Morgan Richard Olivier is an American best-selling author, advocate, and speaker. With a passion for writing that serves as a form of therapy for both herself and her audience – Morgan's outlet for expression fosters and supports conversations that are needed to stop stigmas and support healing, self-acceptance, and personal growth. Since publishing her first book *Questions, Christ, and the Quarter-Life Crisis* in 2020, she has gone to publish four best-selling poetry and prose collections: *Blooming Bare* (2021), *The Tears That Taught Me* (2022), and *One Still Whisper* and also *The Strength That Stays* both in 2023. Morgan has become a source of encouragement and empowerment to both men and women worldwide. Through empathy and wisdom from lessons learned, she enlightens and inspires others to find the greater purpose in life's pains and pressures. Morgan's goal is to crush the image and pursuit of perfection by captivating the raw beauty of sincere progress.

FACEBOOK
@modernmorgan

INSTAGRAM
@modernmorgan

TIKTOK
@morganrichardolivier

YOUTUBE
@modernmorgan

the
freedom
of
forward

www.morganrichardolivier.com

ISBN: 979-8-9857311-6-3

Editor: Carla Dupont
Cover Art: Morgan Richard Olivier
Interior Design: Morgan Richard Olivier
Author Photo: Lori Lyman

Made in United States
Orlando, FL
27 September 2024

52038945R00145